Psyche of Money

Here is How We Are Misled All about the Idea of Money

Author
RAJU SINGH

Editor
Sheen. S. Shashi

Cover designer
AMAN RANCHAN

© All rights reserved

Text copyright reserved with

Raju Singh

The contents of this book may not be reproduced, duplicated or transmitted without direct written permission from the Author

Acknowledgement

Thank you, Aman, for taking the pain of designing the book cover, in spite of rush and deadlines in your business you helped me yet another time to complete yet another book, Thanks for your constant support and availability.

Thanks, Sheen for taking your time for reviewing and editing, I can understand the amount of time you spent in reviewing and correcting the errors. Thanks for helping me bring this book live.

Dedication

I would like to dedicate this book to my family, classmates, college friends, colleagues and students for their love, support and trust in me

Contents

Introduction..P#1-3

Here is how Gold come To the Market............................P#4-6

Here Where All of It Started with I Owe You (IOU)........P#7-8

Here comes the Legitimate Paper Gold............................P#9-12

Here why Money Is Just a Fiction....................................P#13-14

Here Bubble Burst..P#15-17

Here Is How Money Is Created In Modern Banking........P#18-22

Here Is Why Money Doesn't Matter but Value Does.......P#23-30

About The Author

Psyche of Money
Here is How We Are Misled All about the Idea of Money

Introduction

In My first book titled "DEMONITISATION; FIFTY DAYS BETWEEN CASHLESS TO LESS CASH ECONOMY " I tried to describe life and events that had occurred after the announcement of taking off Rs 1000 and Rs 500 notes from India market on 8th November 2016 , in order to wipe off black money market , counterfeit currency and terrorism.

Demonetisation exercise was a well narrated operation to move Indian cash centered economy to the digital economy. But how far has this been achieved is still a topic of hot debate that no one want to debate about. I wonder on ambiguity of my purse each time I pay in cash and stair my mind to answer if it can about the fact, Have I really made it? Are we a cashless or a less cash?

Money is the second best conception that has fascinated me ever after first Love that I eventually let that go after realizing the fact that "No means no and love "can still be platonic.

Economics was never been my favorite subject in the classroom in my school days and seriously I never ever dare to touch economics books in my schools and during my college days however life been a very good professor of economics for me.

Money is a very specific term in economy and has sure certain process to earn and obtain through number of economic activities .Being in the bottom the line I see this very scientific tool too emotionally and psychologically rather than the fact what it has to the mass, I see what it has to do with me?

Being a child I always have this question tickling around in my mind how money is created. Who got the power to create money and If government have that power and if it is pitching the so high on development then why they can't throw the bags full of money and the whole nation becomes rich but then I realized that if that so then no one would even go to work! This has then make me think that the money is produced by means of work (and I should work hard to earn it) but then with the time and age I learnt that this (concept/ideology) is the great trick (game) which works for Bankers and powerful politicians to trick our real work (services /labour/intellect/Grains/skill) into their lockers and credit it whenever they need our services.

This book is inspired by an animated documentary Title" Money as debt" by Canadian Film maker filmmaker Paul Grignon a documentary about the monetary systems practiced through Modern Banking.

In this book I have looked into the mysterious process of the creation of money and how the real money is being replaced merely by a paper/ digital representation of money which are nothing but just promises and how iconic figure has taken over the real value of money that we make upon toil.

In the book I will try to get into the root of money creation and to dig out a very simple answer to the question that had recently started tickling on my head, if my sweat is as good as gold why is that I am not paid in gold, silver or anything that has the real value based on basic principal of economics i.e. demand and supply like any other commodity in the market place?

CHAPTER ONE

Here is how Gold came to the market

I did come across this story in a documentary series named Money as debt available at You tube, a few days back when I was trying to figure out the whole concept of Money and the money market.

I always had the curiosity about whole of Money business right from the childhood about how it is produced?

Here it goes to the history where people used to trade in the market with real objects and skills they possess in return with the objects or Skill they lacked.

Sometime earlier, pretty much anything was used as money, it just required to be portable enough and people had to have faith that later it could be exchanged for things of real value such as food, clothing and shelter. Shells, pretty stones, coco beans even feather which is been used as money.

Like if someone wants to buy a young and healthy buffalo for milk and someone else has it, the former will give something as a token, like a feather or a coco bean as a promise to return young buffalo in future when the later demands it. These tokens were similar to an agreement paper today.

It is pretty much in villages even today. People do exchange Cow buffalo and paddy and wheat, milk etc. upon a promise that the other will return it on time agreed. This happens in case like if Ramesh's buffalo stopped milking and the Sandeep has milk in abundance, Sandeep agrees to provide milk to Ramesh till Ramesh's buffalo get breeded and by the time Sandeep's Buffalo stop milking and he would return the milk.

Coming back to the ancient times where people used to exchange real objects and skill with the same.

Like the value of a glass of water near river cannot be the same as the glass of water in the desert as the value of sand in the desert cannot be same as the value of sand in the snow mountain. The value of object is determined by the efforts one make to bring the object/good/service in the market. This is where money is created as real value depending upon the effort one makes to complete the trade.

But there was a problem in this as the value of the objects and skills are undefined and often disputed among the traders as both parties argues on whose value is greater and who will get more of other in return.

They sorted this out by coming to the conclusion that they will set up a particular value against all Goods and services with mutual agreement and will trade (exchange) depending on the demand and the availability of the object with the objects/metal / service that are already recognized as valuables among all of them.

Gold was as a precious metal in those days as much as today so everyone accepted gold a means of exchange and standard units of gold is been moulded and everyone started trading in gold.

The price of all goods against each unit of gold (coin) are set and agreed among everyone and the trade flow as smoothly as never before as the gold coins were welcomed by everyone without any resistance which led to high liquidity in transitions and flawless trading.

CHAPTER TWO

Here where all of it started with I Owe You (IOU)

In the previous chapter, I wrote on how the Gold came to the market and eased the daily transactions of trade activities.

The traders were treading their products (Grains, clothes, etc.) Labour and skills in returns with the Gold coins against the standardized price of possessions/goods which were set in a mutual agreement among all.

This raised the volume of gold circulation in the market which in turn increased the risk of theft and violent incidents as people did not have secure place to store this precious metal.

There were also the risks involved in the transportation of huge amount of gold from one city to other city for trade/payments because of unsafe journey through Jungles which were safe haven for Dacoits who then found an easy way of making money by looting Merchants and travellers passing by these dark Jungles.

Here comes an idea of a Bank which instantly everyone banked upon.

Here the goldsmith comes into the rescue, as the goldsmiths had been trading in gold from years they are the experts in trading and handling gold. They had secure lockers to protected by guards he promised traders to provide safe lockers for their gold and valuables by keeping small part from the deposit as a service charge and a promise to return the gold whenever traders want it back (very few asked for the return though) by showing that promissory note /an agreement with the details of the amount of gold coins deposited in the bank agreed / understood by both the parties (Bank and trader here)

Since this new place (Bank) was highly protected by armed soldiers, it attracted most of the traders for whom it's seems to be a fair deal and a great way for securing their gold and life.

The traders welcomed this whole new concept where they no longer had to worry about the safety of the gold and started depositing the gold to the bank.

With the promissory note (an agreement having details of their gold deposit) they started paying and accepting as a payment of their trade.

This was even more convenient in carriage and transportation without any risk as these were only pieces of paper.

Hence soon all of the gold (most of the gold) has been replaced by the promissory notes (IOU papers) duplicating the amount of real Gold deposited in the bank (or otherwise fake paper Gold).

CHAPTER THREE

Here comes the Legitimate Paper Gold

By now we all know how the barter system was replaced by Gold trading and about how the limitations of gold trading due to fear of loot and theft resulted in transactions via goldsmith's (Bank's) promissory notes otherwise known as IOUs issued by Banks by now (Lockers owned by Goldsmiths) as a receipt of the gold deposited in their lockers (Bank).

The trade got liquefied even better and the market started operating in exchange of these IOUs which were even accepted in great distant markets without any objections as people were assured that these paper receipts are equivalent to gold and they can get the gold from the goldsmith whenever they like to take it.

This made trade more diverse and helped business to widen its reach across the extended territories with enormous growth possibilities in trade and commerce literally anywhere in the world.

Fair until the goldsmith were signing promissory notes equaling the amount of gold deposited in their locker (bank)); Say for an example for each gold coin, one promissory note, it was a fair trade and a fair promise.

But by Looking at the trend of the market the goldsmith observed over years that the traders who were depositing the gold were rarely turning bank to the bank for asking their gold and on the other hand there were potential capable lenders (With mortgage) who were coming to the banks asking for the money for conducting trade with a promise of returning in future with additional amount as an interest.

Goldsmith has taken this opportunity very well, knowing this fact the not all who deposited the gold would turn up at same time even if some come and ask for the gold, he started signing receipts for the gold which were not even there in the locker. In other way we can say that he signed the IOUs against the gold already deposited and against which the IOU is already been signed and out in the market.

They lend these receipts (Money by now) to the borrower against the "Will" to surrender the mortgage (grain, land, animals) agreed by the borrower by the time of agreement in a specific time of return.

They also kept monitoring the trend of deposit and lending closely so that they would be able to justify the promise whenever the trader did feel to get return of the gold. (Among few who ask for the gold return)

Say for each gold coin if the goldsmith had signed even one extra receipt; to be very fair both of the notes should come back to the Banks to get the real Gold out of the bank and this never happened neither the lander (Owner of the gold) nor the borrower went to the bank asking for the gold at the same time and the borrower's receipt (note) in fact is no different than the lender's receipt (note) both of the receipt as these receipt were signed in the same way in the same paper. People hardly have any idea of this trend as they felt that the goldsmith is trading with his own gold.

Goldsmith enjoyed this new power of creating paper gold by doing nothing but signing fake paper gold (IOUs) with the value exactly as same to the real Gold.

His only turmoil was to find capable borrowers (who were readily available) ready to borrow these fake gold having at least some real objects as mortgage and a "Will" to lose them if they failed to return back the paper gold on time as agreed by both the parties (Goldsmith and the borrower here).

In this way Goldsmith won real over fake and since there were quite a large number of capable borrowers who were interested in borrowing these fake paper gold (without even knowing what they are borrowing is just papers) by surrendering their real object to the Goldsmith in this way grow richer, fatter and powerful.

The other implication of this lending system was the invisible effects in the market.

As these fake paper gold were same as in appearance and looks and also carries the same value as of the real Gold , Goldsmith easily injected these fake currencies (against which no real Gold existed in the locker) in the market through the borrowers without leaving a slightest hint for the traders.

As these notes were having the same buying capacity that of real note (signed against the real Gold) the trade in the market remained unaffected and the fake notes undetected.

CHAPTER FOUR

Here why Money is just a Fiction

Now that the Goldsmith got the very idea of making money out of thin air and there were traders who wanted to extend their trade, there happened to be a demand of credit and the bank had taken this opportunity a step ahead by making credit available to the potential trader capable of repaying these credit with additional money otherwise known as interest.

It's interesting to understand Interest here, Frist of all let's see what an Interest is? It's the additional amount of money that one needs to pay on loan amount. It's absolutely simple until we know the source of this additional money?

Let's assume that the bank lend me one gold coin (real physical gold coin of a certain weight in case of real transaction) and asked me to pay a gold coin weighing slightly higher than the coin, the additional weight an interest the bank had levied upon me, as fair as it seems but how will I get the additional weight of gold that is not even in existence?

In ancient times charging any interest on loan was called usury subjected to severe punishment which may include even death. Every major religion forbids usury. Most of the argument made against the practice was held that the money's only legitimate purpose is to facilitate the exchange of real good and services. Any form of money making money for simply having money was regarded as an act of a parasite or of a thief however it's the credit needs when the commerce increased the argument eventually gives way to the argument that the lending involves risk of loss of opportunity to lander and therefore attempting to make a profit from landing is justified.

Today these notions seem equate. Today the idea of making money from money is held as an ideal way to strive for "why work when you get our money to work for you?"

Now to understand this more let's suppose there is a sustainable economy restrict itself to the present day income and the money system based on a real value. This further implies there is as much of money as there is resource ;Since the sole purpose of money is to facilitate the transition of real good and services it should not be more than the resource in actual. Say if we have one hammer we cannot have two hammers on the paper (representation of hammer) like the story of the gold smith I wrote before that he landed money as receipt/ clean check against the gold that was not in real existence.

Further if few people in system begin systematically to lend the money at an interest, their share of the money supply will grow. If they continue this, and all the money they get paid back what's the inevitable result? The money lenders will end up with all the money!!! And thereafter, when the foreclosure and bankruptcy are filed they will get over real property too.

CHAPTER FIVE

Here Bubble Burst

Now that we have slight idea of history of money let's get into the real business of banks and the mechanism of creating money out of nothing and the irony is that very few of us know the real business of bank.

Let's further go into the past, now we know that how goldsmith was injecting false credit in the market which were nothing but paper of promise of gold that the goldsmith made in return after showing up their receipts but in actual there was not as much of gold as there were receipts floating in the market.

This had made the goldsmith richer and richer and he started enjoying the absolute power and full control of creating money and hence the value as of real things and services were exchanged over this fake paper gold.

Suspicion start growing and few of the rich business men had started realizing the source of enormous wealth of the goldsmith. Now they started demanding their real gold upon depositing those receipts of promise and slowly the news spread and more people and traders started showing up in the bank asking for the deposited gold but the fact was there was no gold as much of the receipts and hence goldsmith and the bank broke down. . This is otherwise known as run on the bank.

Now since the credit was utterly necessary for the new trades and taxes collected by these trades contributes to a good portion of state funds the ruler/ government made banks as the legal profitable financial institute and also passed the bill that bank can provide credit to the market in the ratio of 1:10, that mean bank can lend ten paper gold if they have one unit of real gold in their vault. This was the small feet into the door hence the beginning of an era of modern banking and bank credit

The world has been through several financial crises until now and the biggest of all was the great depression which stared during 1929 and lasted until 1941. This is the longest, deepest and the most widespread depression of 20th century.

The depression originated from US by the sudden down fall of stock market and affected most of country. The shear prices were drastically declined and this caused closure of main stream work place like production factories and ultimately millions of job loss.

Economists have vivid arguments on the cause of great depression. Some argued that it was the direct result of stock market collapse however others see the stock crash as a symptom rather than a cause. Amid varied arguments, one of the interesting reasons of this economic downfall purposed by contemporary economists was that the Federal Reserve had almost hit the limit of the approved credit limit that could be backed by the gold in its Possession.

At that time the amount of credit Federal Reserve could issue was limited by the Federal Reserve Act which required 40% gold backing of Federal Reserve Notes issued. This implies that the Federal Reserve can issue bank notes of one million dollar on every four hundred thousand worth gold in its vault. To clarify this further, it's legal for the Federal Reserve to print six hundred thousand dollar without any possession of actual value like Gold or any asset. However during great depression even this limit was hit and the money supply (promissory notes) in the market was far more than the actual gold in the vault.

This had dropped money supply in the market as the Federal Reserve cannot print bank notes as the limit had exhausted. Further a "promise of gold "is not as good as "Gold in the hand", particularly when they only had enough gold to cover 40% the "Gold promise" floating in the market".

To put check on this in 1933, President Rooseveit signed Executive Order6102 making the private ownership of Gold certificates, coin and bullion illegal, this had propelled commoner to surrender their gold holding. In this way the gold reservoir were refilled and hence this enabled Federal Reserve to bring more credit in the market with new currency, hence market liquidities liquidates.

CHAPTER SIX

Here is how money is created in modern banking

We are been taught from our early days about the importance of money and how we should behave with it. "Every penny saved is a penny earned" which is a simple philosophy that majority of the intellectual kid follows

This philosophy is deeply rooted in our sub conscious and we are made to believe firmly that saving money for when its rain is the best practice a wise man should follow which then becomes a key for the modern banking and the monetary system worldwide.

Banks capitalizes on this social mindset to get into the business and dominates entire societies across the world which on the surface seem to be largely political but it's isn't. It's the economics that dominates the goodwill and politics is just a puppet in the hands of those who has the power of generating money.

Most of us know that the money is created by government however if I say it's only a small proportion of fait money is created by the government and the rest of money in the world economic system doesn't exist at all, I know there would be very few who would like to take this statement. Let me try to illustrate how it is.

We at the very young age are encouraged to save money in fancy piggy banks and when it's full, then it's believed to be paramount and cool to put this money in the bank, thus owning a bank account, and of course who doesn't wants to have a bank account?

Over the years we believe the figures shown in the bank account is our money in the bank but it actually isn't. We deposit the money we saved with the feeling that we can get it back whenever we want it back. But it's not the money that we are going to get back but it just a promise in whichever form it may seems it may the digital figure that showing on our bank account or on the piece of paper that we call bank check, it's just trade of promises There is difference between Money and the promise that is soon to revel.

In common usages the term deposit means to set something down but the use of the word deposit with refer to bank is misleading. Bank deposit in reality is a loan and the amount of money in our bank account really indicates how much money the bank owes us. In the records, bank promises to pay us our money, not exactly the money that we deposited. The truth is when we hand our money from the piggy bank to the bank our money becomes the banks money and gets leverage to do whatever with it as it pleases. All of the money in the bank is their money and not ours that way the bank, pays interest on the money we deposited in the bank. We know that we can go any time at the bank and take out our money out in cash if we want to which seems very logical and fair practice until we understand the difference between actual money and the a promise to pay money.

What happens in bank effect every one yet few of us know anything at all how banking works. The entire world economy runs on banks credit created out of nothing and when that credit system breaks down every one suffers. To make things worse the explanation provided for this breakdown by experts has never looked at the root cause. Mainly that the other than cash and coins, which make up one to five percentage in the circulation , all the money in existence today is created out of principal of the bank loan . Banks requiring principle plus interest is so called repayment. Not only does this makes existence of money entirely dependent on the availability of bank credit, it makes the system as a whole bankrupt by design as total debit principal plus interest exceeds total assets the system had created In reality there is only 5 % of the money in the circulation which is fait money and the rest is bank credit from the moment first loan document is signed.

Before going further I would like to throw more light on what's wrong in the bank promise to pay and the money that we deposited in the bank. How do we get money? By earning it, by putting real effort and create real value in terms of real objects and services. But how does the bank earn money, by simply creating it out of thin air.

Let's see how the money is created out of credit with a simple example, Ramesh is working in a firm on a fair amount of salary that credits at a specific day at the end of the month. Now he wants to own a car and there is the other person say Abdul wants to sell his car let's assume that the price of the car Abdul made on offer is Rs 10,000 but Ramesh do not have a lump sum to pay the amount to Abdul however Ramesh has confidence that if bank provide this lump sum now he will return this amount to the bank in portion over a period of time. So he applies for a loan in a bank near him.

Bank upon verification of Ramesh ability to repay this amount in future with principle and interest welcomes as its new customer. On approval the bank create an account for Ramesh and types in the bank owe Rs 10,000. This Rs.10,000 is not taken from anywhere it's created on the spot, it's just few strokes on the keyboard and the figures appears on the account page of Ramesh. The borrower doesn't take this money in cash instead he writes check on his account to buy the car. Seller then deposit this newly created Rs 10,000 in his bank (Remember the story of goldsmith, where he used to provide loan to the potential borrower receipts of the gold that was not at all existent in his vault? Say for every gold coin there was more than 10-15 gold receipt out in the market? But this practice made legal in the modern banking supplying with the logic that credit is necessary for the operation of trade however a monetary agency (federal reserve in US , Reserve bank of India) to keep check to maintain this ratio at 1:9, means bank is allowed to make loan of 9 dollars against each one dollar in its vault) now at ratio of 9:1 this 10,000 deposit allows the sellers bank to create new loan of 9,000. This deposit by the third party (Seller-Abdul) becomes the legal basis to third issue of bank credit. This time the amount of 8100 in this way each new deposit contains the potential of slightly smaller loan in a decreasing series new in stage however the money taken from the bank in cash and if not deposited in the bank the process stops. That's the unpredictable part of the money creation mechanism but more likely at every step new bank credit money will be deposited in a bank and the reserve ratio process can repeat itself over and over to almost a hundred thousand of brand new bank credit money is been created in the banking system. This newly generated money is been created entirely from debt and all transaction is been carried out in bank credit. None of the bank involved need to use the cash in their vault. In this ingenious system the books of each bank and chain must show that the bank has ten percent more on deposit than is out on loan. This gives bank a real good incentive to seek deposit in order to be able to make loan supporting the general people but misleading impression that the loan comes out of deposit. Now it can't be said that any one bank can multiply the initial 10,000 of bank credit to 100,000 of bank credit, however the banking system is a closed loop bank credit created in one bank become deposit at other bank and so on and so on.

In theoretical world of perfectly equal exchanges the bank would owe each other nothing at the end of the day and the 10,000 created out of the thin air loan by the first bank indeed becomes almost a hundred thousand of new loan money in the banking system.

CHAPTER SEVEN

Here is why money doesn't matter but Value does

Money is the measurement by which the goods are valued, the value by which goods are exchanged and in which contracts are made payable, everything receives a value from its use and the value is raised, according to its quality, quantity and demand, Money is not the value by which they are exchanged but the value by which they are exchanged

John Law, Political economist 1705

    The sole purpose of money is to complete the transaction of trade between goods and services. Now we have an idea of how money is been created out of thin air in terms of bank credits in the modern banking system, 95 % of the total money in existence is the bank credits which are noting but the bubble created of a simple universal banking formula of 9:1 which sometimes goes up to 33:1 depending upon the nature of the bank credits. This implies the amount of money in existence is far greater than the actual gold in the vaults of the central banks of the nation. So we if demand the gold with all money we held in cash would never be fulfilled. In fact in 1971 the Us president had passed a bill stating the money would be no longer credited in gold the biggest irony for the people those who thinks the money is valued against gold.

Like time, weight, kilometer money is a measurement of the real good and services in the real physical world, but how come the existence of money is in far abundance then the Goods and services itself?

Let's try to look deeper into the current monetary design, In present bank credit and money system, the principal amount of bank loan is simply created from the borrower's promise to pay bank the principle plus interest in money but the money to pay the interest is not created and therefore it is mathematically impossible to pay off all debt however its only when all loan are concurrent the money and the interest are paid back in lump sum. But that's not the banking system works in general. A Bank loan usually gets paid in a series of payment over a period of time.

Money is both the stock of the amount of money in any time and the flow of transaction money is used for. Flow is the real measure of economic activity; it's much more significant than the stock in the money system as it multiplies effective money in the circulation. It works like this, if rich men lend one Rupee to someone and that's the only Rupee in existence in the stock, can someone pay him back the hundred rupees? If it had to be pay in one lump sum? The other 99 rupees interest on the loan (one rupee here) would be impossible to pay, it would be impossible to pay even two rupee because there is only one rupee in existence. However the rich man let him/her pay hundred rupees in one rupee payment, magic happens in fact in one rupee payment you could pay any amount of interest on the loan ,the only condition required to make the full payment of hundred rupees with only one rupee in existence ,(did not understand this. We need to talk if you gets the opportunity to earn or otherwise get that rupee back each time you pay to the lander. This is the flow, by means of flow the same one rupee can paid any number of times becomes effectively huge amount of cash, all legitimately represent the work done to earn them. It's always the work, real value that pays back the debt and gives the rupee its value not the rupee itself. The relationship in this argument is awfully unequal because the man with money has enslaved the man without it.

The simple loan in interest need not produce shortage of money or cause unpayable debt if the flow is hundred percent as in the example. Flow is the real measure of real economic activities, it's much more significant to the stock in the money system as it multiplies the effective money in the circulation given that today we use exclusively debt money system. What is flowing in all these transactions is bank credits or promises to pay money? This credit is nothing more than the promise to pay this credit back usually according to a time she dual and usually with the interest added. To pay this credit back most us will have to earn by productive work. Therefore the real value of money that flows in our economy today is created by our promises of future productive work. We take a loan to have something now rather than later, we agree to pay the interest on into the future thus reducing our spending power often by the interest more than the original loan however by the understanding for flow we see that there is no arithmetic problem with the charging of interest. The problem is social and systematic lenders neither has obligation nor incentive to spend their interest income so that borrowers can earn it again and again, in fact money lent ones into existence is lent is lent as existing money second and the third time in expectation for more gain. The problem is basically one of incomplete recycling; Money needs to be spent, earned and use to extinguish the debt that created it. It is instead lent and invested for gain. In other words the money that must be ideally should have extinguished, is instead expected to grow forever. This is the universal mechanism functions in the world's banking institutions.

Here is the other example of basic mechanism inherent to all lending let's say I have lent you hundred rupees and you spent it in the circulation its eventually ends up in possession of someone who doesn't need to spend it and decides to lend it instead , now once again let's say this is only 100 rupees in existence so you have to borrow from the secondary in order to pay off your debt to me but now you have to lent it from me to pay off the secondary lender, this twice lent money has become a perpetually unpayable debt . This debt can never be extinguished or reduced without a default notice that interest doesn't even enter in the equation. The problem is perpetual debt remains whether interest or not and even if the money is of an intrinsic value such as gold or silver or it is issued by government as cash , twice lent money create perpetual debt exactly the same way .

Now, when the same money is lent several times with interest simultaneously not as the debt perpetual society as a whole is paying money lender multiples of the interest rates for the use of the same money. There is an expectation that the debt money to increase indefinitely by been lent to the interest but this requires us to mentally divorce the money from which it came however the reality is every dollar/ rupees created today has a scheduled appointment to be extinguished as a principal payment of the loan that created it and that way debt money can't be separated from the debt that created it. This is like yo -yo spun into the economy and pulled back in the appointed time. In order to the yo- yo to be freely returned returning, all of the debt money needs to extinguish and debt has to be available to be earned, in short the flow must be complete.

In current bank credit system money is created is debt to banks , this debt is required to be paid in money either fait cash(money issued by government) or bank credit, therefor the ability of all borrowers to repay depends upon the availability of fait cash or bank credit. The supply of fait cash is controlled by the nation's central bank but fait cash makes up a very small proportion of money, usually the 95% of all money is bank credit which is controlled by the bank itself. Bank can constrict the supply of bank credit anytime they want to with higher interest rate or not granting loan. On the other hand bank can lower interest rate and encourage borrowing but they can't increase the money supply unless borrowers are willing to borrow.

At this point we have basic idea of how money is just some figure a number and how we are being misled that the money in the circulation is the representation of the amount of actual gold in the vault of central bank, in fact the total amount of cash in the economy is noting nothing but just the bubble formed by bank credits which are no more the promises of money that are not actually in the reservoirs of bank. These bank credits are then flowed in the economy and made available to be earned by means of real work. These credits are no different than the counterfeit currencies in the market which get dissolved in the economy when not detected and function same as money but when detected is subjected to severe punishment for the people who create it ,how come the money created out of the thin air have no real basis different from counterfeit currencies?

We have looked into an example in the previous chapter where a loan of Rs 10,000 for Ramesh had created an opportunity for the other loan tractions to create Rs 100,000 of brand new money on at the end of fewer transition through various banking loans with a universal banking process of 9:1. What we do not know is there is no actual money involved in the total traction; In fact the bank didn't even have money to lend at all. It's just the figures showing in the account and we sign cheque against those figures that we call our money in the bank are just the promises to pay by means for productive work. These cheques are accepted everywhere no body questions and refuses to be paid in those cheques however what if someone refused to be paid in check or fait currencies or electronic transfer? What's wrong if I ask my payment be in Gold, silver or any things that has real value, I know this cannot be realistic but I just wonder of universal law of creating money, whosoever has taken the responsibly to create should ensure that the money created in the system should be exactly of same value of the real things in the system. It should not exceed resources. The second thing need to be think about is why money is a single commodity valued against single parameter i.e. Gold why it can't be anything in real or the future productive work? There are waves of economists who are opposing this monopolistic idea of creating money as debt and have proposed theories on alternative money which is purely based on recycling of money.

One of such system alternative is self-issued credit. As per the system individual could issue their own credit on the base of their existing product and services or on the future productive work and allow it to exchange in the market ,speculation would transform from an endeavor to suck money out of transacting to add value to existing relationship and the people would be free to refuse specific credit that had been issued by specific businesses , giving total control of individuals to choose what group of businesses they are willing to support .

Self-issued credit is not a new idea, during Middle Ages self-issued credits were issued by anyone who produced a good or provided a service backing for their money in other words self-issued credit represent the good and service in the market.

I am going to describe self-issued credits and number of alternative money proposed by various modern economists in my next book "Green Economy –Alternative currencies "where we will look into the possibility of fair money system and how the people of the countries like Greece, USA and those are going through economic down fall are embracing methodology of money system parallel to the present monetary system which are based on real value like real goods and services not on the speculations and bubbles from the controlled system of world banking based on a simple narrative of scarcity and fulfillment.

About The Author

The author is freelance writer and self-publisher. Being born in Rajasthan and bought up in the north-eastern hills of India he has experienced and learned multi-cultural lifestyle, diversified Indian geographical landscape and beliefs that hold this large country together as a whole.

Being raised up in various regions of the country, he has learnt the art of interaction with people and landscapes that represents the diverse socio-economic structures and traditions.

He has wide experience of writing and producing radio programs as he has worked as program producer and Station manager in various FM Radio stations across Far-Western Nepal during the period of democratic transition in Nepal

Other Books by Author

Demonitisaton; Fifty Days between Cashless to Less Cash Economy: A Journey from an electronic wallet to return of a bank note

Toxic Love; Not a Love Story: Dark Secrets of Emotional Parasites

Please do share how you feel about this book; I'd really appreciate it if you would post a short review on Amazon. Your support really does make a lot of difference and I do read all the reviews personally so that I can get your feedback and make this book even better. These reviews are a great way for communication between a subject and a reader and this interaction opens wide range of possibilities for new thoughts and ideas to bud and grow

Please write to me at authorrajusingh@Gmail.com

Thanks for your support

www.ingramcontent.com/pod-product-compliance
Lightning Source LLC
Chambersburg PA
CBHW031514210526
45464CB00007B/2910